D1553901

WIN
WITH NUMEROLOGY

A
NUMEROSCOPE
HANDBOOK

By Myrtle K. H. Bradley

DeVORSS & CO., *Publishers*
P.O. Box 550
Marina del Rey, CA 90294

2nd Printing, 1985

ISBN: 0-87516-482-X
Library of Congress Card Catalog Number: 82-70776

Printed in the United States of America

CONTENTS

FOREWORD

Numerology?

What has 1, 2, 3, 4, 5, 6, 7, 8, 9 got to do with *your* life?

A complete stranger calls Myrtle Bradley. He has heard of her through friends. He asks for a "reading." Myrtle requests only three bits of information on the phone: name at birth, present name, birthdate.

Later when the person arrives at her door for the appointed reading, she invariably greets him with a fond remark as though she had known him for years. Now, while Myrtle is an uncommonly friendly person, part of her "old friends" attitude is that she *does* know the person—knows in which areas he is most adept, the troubling areas of his life, the future context for challenge he will face. How?

The magic of numbers—those democratic digits which she brilliantly interprets for each unique individual; those faithful numbers that tell the eternal story of human progress.

This deceptively simple and calmly written little volume begins with the statement "Success is our goal in life.'' It continues with every word carefully chosen. Not one is extraneous. The author, my mentor and source of endless encouragement, refers to more than material success. Her purpose in sharing her thirty years of numerological experience (in the last third of her 85 years) is to increase every reader's emotional, physical, spiritual and material success.

Through interpreting the significant numbers in our numeroscope we can focus on, tune into and get a grasp on what we have been up to and where we are going.

Members of the intelligentsia may find it hard to accept that numbers can shine more light on their lives' patterns than years of therapy, religious study or complex intellectual systems. They may not cotton to being known on the basis of ''mere'' numbers. Yet those who respect the fundamental nature of things, the mysteriously miraculous workings of the cosmos, are happy to learn about themselves from Myrtle's clear, concise and workable presentation of numerology. She does not ''make up'' anything; she merely throws light on what is there.

Numerology is an artistic science, or a scientific art, which is coming into its own again in this transition phase of human development. Beset on all sides by grievous planetary and personal problems, numerology as put forth here can be used to get the ''big picture.'' Ignore the opportunity at your peril!

This book is for teenagers and for persons as old as the author herself; for Hispanics, Iranians, Blacks and Croatians; for people who attended school to 8th grade and those who have advanced degrees; for people who are "lucky" and for those who have not yet reached their goals.

As you travel the road of life, is your attention on the rearview mirror, or are your hands on the steering wheel? Numerology reinforces your *choice* in the matter. Read the book through first to get a feel for the concepts, working out your own numbers. Since interpretation is at least half the art, use the numbers that are significant for you in the way Myrtle does, to release your potential and positivity. Then have fun using numbers with family, friends, famous people, historical figures. Caution: get your numbers right or you'll be telling Tom's story to Harry and Mary's to Margaret!

Myrtle K. H. Bradley has been pivotal in the lives of hundreds of people who are questing, open, positive spirits, people who are looking for information to support their growth. If you picked up this book, you are one of them.

Lest you think the 85-year-old author a nice little old lady, probably somewhat crotchety, perhaps bent over and surely frail, I hasten to let you know that she retains the figure and most of the stamina that made her the top San Francisco fashion model in the 20s, has a quick laugh and keen sense of humor, and is as sensitive and responsive as anyone would hope to be at the peak of aliveness. Two hours in her undemanding company are enough to recharge this writer's batteries for a month.

The beauty of this book is that its wisdom is the result of a full, full 85 years of living combined with the indisputable usefulness of our friends, the numbers. As one whose life's work "took wings" because of the reading Myrtle gave me, I enthusiastically commend this volume to you.

Barbara S. F. Davis
(Nine Air)

WIN WITH NUMEROLOGY

"Fortune beckons us—
win with Numerology
in the game of life!"

Success is our goal in life. To attain success seems effortless to a very few only. To some it becomes a ceaseless, interminable struggle. Many give up. Others plod on. Yet there are ways to make the path easier. Numerology, the vibration of numbers, applied to our birthdate and given name at birth, plus any acquired or assumed names at a later date, when understood and put to work positively by our own minds, can and does perform miracles for us.

I was first introduced to numerology in 1949 when I met Louise Snyfeld, a practicing numerologist, who guided and taught me over the years. Her system, an ancient one, was learned from an East Indian. All the modern books on the subject, so far as I have been able to trace, have neglected to include the use of the Money or Success number which she stressed emphatically and

1

which I have found works like magic to assist people in gaining their goals.

Also in said books, nothing has been mentioned concerning the Spiritual Calendar and Spiritual Birthdays, two of the most potent weapons to wield in the war for success. This is the reason I have succumbed to the pressure of my many friends to put these ideas into written form for availability to those who wish to improve their lives.

Another precept that Louise stressed vigorously was to *learn* and *apply* the *basics* of numerology but to avoid becoming involved in extended detail for the reason that our purpose in using the art is to help us to advance toward our goals. When we become bogged down in petty detail the science rules us. We are no longer in the driver's seat; just too busy trying to figure out what the hour-to-hour, minute-to-minute influences are. For this reason I shall make this discourse as simple and concise as possible while still giving as complete a working guide as necessary to further your progress.

We shall start with a Table of Tools and Terms so that you may readily understand the nomenclature of the numeroscope.

TABLE OF TOOLS AND TERMS

"Without tools and terms
thoughts are in a quandary—
Clear the deck, then sail!"

1. Digits: Numbers 1, 2, 3, 4, 5, 6, 7, 8, 9.

2. Special numbers:
   Master numbers 11, 22, 33.
   Trinity numbers 8, 9, 11.
   Caution or Karmic nos. 13, 14, 16, 19.

3. The Three Signs: Water, Fire, Air.

4. Destiny Number: Total numbers of birthdate reduced to a digit.

5. Expression Number: Total of numbers in given name at birth reduced to a digit.

6. Reality or Power Number: Destiny and Expression numbers added and reduced to a digit.

7. Ambition Number: Total of vowels in given name at birth reduced to a digit.

8. Impression or Personality Number: Consonants in given name at birth reduced to a digit.

9. Cycles:
   Three Major Cycles ruled by digits in birthdate.
   Minor Cycles or Tides—Nine-Year Periods or Personal Years.

10. Pinnacles: Addition of birth digits.

11. Challenges: Subtraction of birth digits.

12. Money or Success Numbers: 5, 8, 6.

13. Spiritual Birthdays and Spiritual Calendar.

14. Numbers of Alphabet:

1	2	3	4	5	6	7	8	9
A	B	C	D	E	F	G	H	I
J	K	L	M	N	O	P	Q	R
S	T	U	V	W	X	Y	Z	&

NUMBERS AS TOOLS
OF NUMEROSCOPE

"Numbers are the tools
with which we build our ladders
to ascend the heights!"

The language of numbers is easy to learn. The application takes practice and perseverance but the results are well worth the effort. I have watched many climb their ladders to success. All who reach the heights glory in the view and encourage others.

The digits, numbers one through nine, plus eleven, twenty-two and thirty-three are the tools of the numeroscope. All numbers in numerology are reduced to a digit with the exception of eleven, twenty-two, and thirty-three, which are called Master numbers and have special connotations explained on page 13.

The manner in which a digit is reached is as follows: Take the year 1981. Add the numbers in the year thus: $1 + 9 + 8 + 1 = 19$. $1 + 9 = 10$. $1 + 0 = 1$, showing that 1981 is a *One* world year.

We apply this method to all numbers in numerology with the exception of the Master numbers 11, 22 and 33. Practically the only instance in which the Master numbers are reduced is in computing the Pinnacles and Challenges.

In addition to the digits and the Master numbers 11, 22 and 33, there are three Destiny numbers that have special significance, 8, 9 and 11, called Trinity numbers (see explanation on pages 42 & 43). Also numbers 13, 14, 16 and 19, termed Caution or Karmic numbers (explained on page 14).

Numbers, like everything in the universe, vibrate to energy. When you understand the import of the various vibrations and apply their influences in your daily activities, your advancement toward whatever goals you set will progress more rapidly and easily.

Before we can map a fascinating and revealing chart, we must understand the various elements that go into assembling the chart. First, the birthdate designates the all-important *Destiny* (month, day and year added and reduced to a digit). The birthdate also fixes the *three Major Cycles* (ruled by month, day and year); the *Minor Cycles* (nine-year periods known as *Personal Years*, 1 to 9, or tides, arrived at by adding your month and day of birth to the current year and reducing to a digit); the *Pinnacles* (helpful highlights); and *Challenges* (tests). The *Day* of birth establishes the *Concord* or *Sign* you are in.

The name reveals the Expression or life path you are on (number vibrations of full name given at birth): the Ambition or Heart's Desire (vowels in name): *Impression* or Personality (consonants). The name also reveals *Temperament* or Mental, Emotional, Physical and Intuitive status.

Before we begin an analysis of the foregoing terms, you will at this point, no doubt, be interested in the various number vibrations and their meanings.

INTERPRETATION OF
NUMBER VIBRATIONS

"Life is a puzzle—
    number vibrations can solve
        its hidden riddles."

The Key to the general influences of each number regardless of its position in a chart as well as its application to the Personal years and to the days, months and years in the Spiritual Calendar is as follows:

Numeral 1. Independence. Self-motivation. Self-reliance. Invention. Pioneering. Activity. Force. Ambition. One denotes a beginning, a time to start new things. A One day in a One Personal Year is the ideal date to schedule a wedding. A One influence is a time to make important contacts or appointments; a time to start a new project or a new job or any drastic change in life style like moving to a new residence or starting a new line of endeavor. One is the strongest number in nine. If it is a person's Spiritual Birthday, it is doubly powerful for such individual.

Numeral 2. Cooperation. Diplomacy. Partnership. Harmony. Detail. Service. Rhythm. This is an excellent vibration for group work. It is not a lively influence, however. Apply yourself to detail or anything that must necessarily be accomplished, but do not push.

Numeral 3. Self-expression. Enthusiasm. Optimism. Humor. Joy. This is a strong vibration. Creative. Artistic. Let the imagination have full sway. Three is an excellent social vibration, a time for entertainment.

Numeral 4. Practicality. Application to work. Concentration. Economy. Patience. Honesty. Loyalty. Four is a down to earth, hard work vibration building a foundation. If you are not doing the thing you like to do or are predestined for in this life span, then work can become drudgery. It is important to express your innate abilities, thus making your efforts a challenge bringing rewards. Four is the roughest number in nine. More accidents occur in a Four vibration than any other. Let caution rule. If Four is your Spiritual Birthday, it affords protection not accorded to others with the exception of Twenty-twos.

Numeral 5. Freedom. Activity. Versatility. Change. Travel. Adventure. Progress. Five is a super-active vibration. Excellent for change and travel. Must guard against too many varied activities which may bring failure through dissipating the energies. If Five denotes the Impression or Personality number, this individual tends to appear youthful and attractive in appearance. If multiple Fives are placed in key positions of a chart, you may be sure the individual concerned is not amenable to suggestions for his conduct. Five is the Money or Success number of the Water sign.

Numeral 6. Home. Domesticity. Service. Responsibility. Six is a beautiful number. A love vibration inspiring thoughts of home, marriage and community interests. It is a strong responsibility vibration urging service to others. There is a negative attribute aligned with Six which must be reckoned with, especially if Six is situated as the Destiny number, the Ambition, Expression or as a Challenge. This quality is the fact that Six believes himself or his attitude in any matter to be absolutely right and everyone who differs to be wrong. He must strive to understand that someone in a different position may see things differently. Also a Six is often inclined to manipulate others for his own gains particularly if multiple Sixes appear in the name and/or Challenges. Six is the Money or Success number of the Air.

Numeral 7. Spirituality. Specialization. Perfection. Research. Analytical. Studious. Wisdom.

Silence. Secretive. Seven leads to introspection, analyzing and perfecting one's undertakngs. Under its influence one is often inclined to withdraw from active participation in events and to turn within to explore possibilities for furthering his progress. Seven is called the Ripening Tide, a period of delays, like waiting for sunshine to ripen fruit. It may be a restless period for many who cannot seem to accomplish their objectives. Relaxation is the order of this Seven influence to avoid frustration while awaiting the following strong Eight influence. Let Nature have her way.

Numeral 8. Harvest. Material Success. Business. Finance. Authority. Management. Executive ability. Efficiency. Eight is the harvest number, the practical devotion to work and its rewards. Too often Eights overlook spiritual values in the scramble for material success. Eight is the Money or Success number of the Fire Sign. If Eight is the Destiny number, then it is also a Trinity number.

Numeral 9. Universality. Leadership. Optimism. Idealism. Drive. Energy. Philanthropy. Service. Nine being the universal number demands dealing with the many instead of being self-centered. Capable of great acheivements especially if it is the Destiny, Expression, Reality or Ambition number. If found as the Impression number it indicates the individual appeals favorably to most people. Nine is a finishing cycle. If it is the Destiny, it is also a Trinity number.

Numeral 11. Idealism. Diplomacy. Tact. Co-operation. Inspiration. Intuition. Invention. Limelight. Eleven is a Master number, also a Trinity number if it is the Destiny. It belongs in a public capacity in the limelight.

Numeral 22. Practical Idealist. Master Builder. Power. Twenty-two, a double eleven, is idealistic but also practical. A Twenty-two vibration can accomplish anything the heart desires. If Twenty-two is the Destiny, then a Four day in the Spiritual Calendar is its Spiritual Birthday offering protection not accorded others in a rough Four vibration except a Four Destiny. If Twenty-two appears as a vibration in one or more of your names, it adds strength and power. Let it work for you.

Numeral 33. This is an extremely high spiritual vibration we are not likely to find as a Destiny number. However, occasionally it shows up as a Reality number (a combination of the Destiny and Expression numbers) in spiritually advanced individuals. It also may appear in a name.

Familiar to all youngsters are TV screen scenarios with the "good guys" and "bad guys." With numbers we also have "bad guys" to confront. These are the Caution or Karmic numbers 13, 14, 16 and 19, which we will now explore. If any one of these numbers is found in key positions in your chart preceding a final digit (13/4, 14/5, 16/7, 19/1) they must be dealt with. The significance of these numbers is the implication that somewhere along the line their negative influences have been indulged instead of overcome.

Numeral 13. The basic vibration that Thirteen suggests is to buckle down to hard work, which, no doubt, was formerly shunned and must now be faced.

Numeral 14. This vibration indicates chiefly a lack of understanding. Many do not understand themselves to say nothing of the motives and actions of others. The practice of meditation is a great help here. Through its regular daily performance we gain insight.

Numeral 16. This number reduces to 7, a spiritual vibration which strongly urges a synergic mode of expression, a balancing of spiritual and material pursuits.

Numeral 19. While Nineteen includes all the numbers, 1 to 9, its basic caution is to handle the strong 1 (independence) in a positive manner. This means to use its leadership to guide and help others, avoiding being domineering toward those less fortunate.

THE THREE CONCORDS OR SIGNS

"Signs pinpoint locales—
we are not adrift alone
in this life's sea lanes!"

Everyone has a special niche in life, a spot
unique to him where he can best work out the
problems that he must solve in order to progress.
Numerology points out the present position of
each of us on the life path through concords or
signs. There are three concords in numerology,
the WATER sign, the FIRE sign and the AIR sign.
The Water sign is known as the scientific concord;
the Fire sign is called the business concord; the
Air sign is termed the artistic concord.

The DAY of birth determines the sign in which
you stand in this lifetime. This material world is a
training school, so to speak, and your complete
birthdate (Destiny) indicates the school grade in
which you are now learning, experiencing or performing, while the calendar *day of birth alone*
signifies the sign you are in.

Anyone born on a One, Five or Seven day, or a
number reducing to 1, 5 or 7 is in the Water sign.

17

Water sign birthdays of any month are 1, 5, 7, 10, 14, 16, 19, 23, 25 and 28.

Those born on a Two, Four or Eight day, or a number reducing to 2, 4 or 8 are in the Fire sign. Fire sign birthdays of any month are 2, 4, 8, 11, 13, 17, 20, 22, 26, 29 and 31.

A birthday on a Three, Six or Nine day, or any number reducing to a 3, 6 or 9 places one in the Air sign. Air sign birthdays of any month are 3, 6, 9, 12, 15, 18, 21, 24, 27 and 30.

Numerology assumes we cannot learn all our lessons in one short lifetime in the physical, material world. We first go through nine phases in the Water sign; then nine in the Fire sign and nine in the Air, repeating in each phase until we have assimilated all necessary data for further progress. If there is anything we have failed to digest properly, we step back to the necessary position or grade to review and pick up the missing knowledge or experience. After completing all the cycles satisfactorily in Water, Fire and Air, we then return in each sign to prove spiritual Sevens. In other words, we must put into practice our spiritual accomplishments to prove our proficiency before advancing to a higher plane of existence. One of the attributes we must acquire and retain is psychic ability. Also we must become healers. The birth of advanced individuals who have already acquired the healing art frequently occurs in a Seven year.

We often find advanced individuals with a birth-date in July, the seventh month, and sometimes on a Seven day like July 7th, 16th or 25th, thereby doubling the seven. This may indicate a final incarnation in this material plane, especially if the Destiny number is Twenty-two and if such an individual lives up to his acquired spiritual accomplishments.

Those standing in the Water sign are most compatible with anyone in their own sign or in the Air sign, while Fire people have greater rapport with other Fire or Air subjects. The Air members intermingle easily with all signs and are particularly inspirational to those in Fire.

However, Fire and Water do not mix. Water puts out Fire but Fire fights back and is difficult to squelch so conflicts arise. Any close relationship like marriage or other partnerships between members of the Water and Fire signs are prone to misunderstandings, often serious conflicts. Such alliances should be shunned unless both parties are advanced enough to cope sensibly with their differences. Understanding numerology and applying its influences is a great help in these situations.

Ofttimes Water subjects become their own worst enemies for the reason that they are inclined to look backwards, dwelling on past mistakes, instead of focusing attention on the path ahead and seeking new opportunities.

THE THREE MAJOR CYCLES

"The Major Cycles
are the steering-gears of life
that point toward our goals."

Whether or not we realize it, number vibrations in our charts are subtly at work steering us in the ways we are meant to go. When we understand the directions they are pointing us, we intensify the action.

The average life span is divided into three major cycles of approximately twenty-five years each. The first cycle comes under the influence of our *month of birth*. The second is ruled by the *digit of our birthday*, and the third cycle by the *digit of our year of birth*. However, there is no hard line of demarcation as the influences are inclined to overlap somewhat.

To calculate the transition from one major cycle to the next we add twenty-five to the year of birth, then figure the *nearest* 1 Personal Year to age twenty-five. Using for example the date July 14, 1950, we add 25 to year 1950 making the total

1975, which reduces to 22. To this we add 7 for July (7th month) and 5 for the 14th day which reduces to 5, thus, $22 + 7 + 5 = 34 = 7$ showing that July 14, 1975, is a 7 Personal Year for this individual. The following year, 1976, would then be an 8 Personal Year, 1977 a 9 Personal Year and 1978 a 1 Personal Year. Therefore 1978 marks the transition from the first major cycle to the second in this birthdate.

To find the change from the second to the third cycle, we follow the same procedure by adding 25 to 1978 (the first transition date) and determining the nearest 1 Personal Year to its total of 2003 which reduces to 5. To this 5 year we then add 5 for the 14th day and 7 for July, thus $5 + 5 + 7 = 17 = 8$, showing 2003 to be an 8 Personal Year, 2004 a 9 and 2005 a 1 Personal Year, the transition date for the third or final cycle.

Since each major cycle embraces such a wide span of time, it is imperative to realize the type of vibration in force for each period so that you may utilize its influence in furthering your progress. Each number indicates the character of activity predominating under its reign. Put its force to work.

For instance, a One cycle—independence, power, strength, etc.; Two—cooperation, partnership, diplomacy; Three—self-expression; Four—practical down to earth application to work; Five—travel, change, much activity; Six—responsibility, domesticity, community projects; Seven—perfection, study, analysis, spirituality; Eight—business and material pursuits; Nine—universality, service to others, completion; Eleven—limelight, invention; Twenty-two—Master Builder, power, extremely strong vibration.

THE MINOR CYCLES OR TIDES

"The Minor Cycles,
    Like ocean tides, ebb and flow,
    help or hinder us."

The Minor Cycles, called Tides, are nine-year periods known as our Personal Years and are influenced by the numbers 1 to 9, each number covering a one-year period from the first of January to the thirty-first of December.

There is a right time for us to forge ahead and a wrong time. You are either in tune or not in tune. You are either magnetically attracting or repelling. This is the influence of your Tides, which you must understand and work with harmoniously.

To determine the influence at work for any particular year or Tide, we reduce the year in question to a digit to which we then add the digits of *month* of our birth and *day* of birth, again reducing to a final digit. For example, take the year 1981, $1 + 9 + 8 + 1 = 19 = 1$, which we find is a 1 year. Now using the birthdate July 14th, July is the 7th month and the 14th day reduces to 5, so we add 1 (year) plus 7 (month) plus 5 (day), which reduces to 4 (1 + 7 + 5 = 13 = 4). Therefore the person with a July 14 birthday is vibrating to a 4 influence in 1981. (See the Four vibration on page 10)

After the middle of the year, the vibration of the next following Tide begins gradually to be felt, becoming stronger as the year advances, reaching the peak at the birth of the New Year.

The most positive vibrations for the Personal Years are the Tides 1, 3, 5, 6, and 8, while either neutral or negative vibrations rule the Tides 2, 4, 7 and 9, 4 being the roughest Tide in nine.

When your Tide is in (positive) direct every possible effort toward your goals. Then when the Tide is out (2, 4, 7, 9) attend to the necessary chores but do not push. Waiting for the next positive Tide will pay off in the long run and you will not have wasted energy.

A One Tide has exceptionally strong positive vibrations; a time to make important appointments, start new undertakings; seek the things you wish to demonstrate in your affairs; a time to start new ventures.

A Two Tide is neutral or slow; a time to do the necessary chores.

A Three Tide is the self-expression vibration, very creative and favorable; an excellent social vibration.

A Four Tide is what my teacher called "vicious" because more accidents are likely to occur, plus other negative conditions in a Four vibration than at any other time. A Four vibration demands caution. Be alert!

A Five Tide is very active; excellent for change and travel.

A Six Tide promotes thoughts of service to others. Home and community interests predominate.

A Seven Tide, called the Ripening Tide, brings many delays in the best laid plans, a time to coast while waiting for the strong Eight Harvest Tide.

An Eight Tide. This is the Harvest tide, a time to reap the benefits for previous efforts. A strong business vibration.

A Nine Tide is a finishing period, a time to clean house by getting rid of things no longer of use to you, winding up loose ends, and preparing for the next Tide which is a strong One, a new beginning.

Only *once* in nine years does one's Spiritual Birthday and Natal birthday fall on the same day. This is like a re-birth, a new beginning, as similar influences prevail as existed at birth. Anyone born in a One year will experience this situation in

1981, which is a One world year. Use these favorable vibrations through the entire year as a revival or new beginning in your affairs.

Whenever the digit of your birth year corresponds with the digit of a current year, you will experience this double birthday to celebrate. Make the most of its favorable vibrations.

THE PINNACLES

"Pinnacles to climb—
  our eyes are on the summit,
    don't let feet be clods!"

Each life is divided into four pinnacles as the earth has four seasons, spring, summer, autumn and winter. The pinnacles designate peaks of influence we may put to work to aid us in furthering our interests, so it is important to understand their vibrations and to apply their positive aspects to daily living. Sometimes seemingly devastating experiences come to us but once they are passed, we can look back and realize they occurred for our own good progress.

A circle, which represents a complete lifetime, contains 360 degrees which we divide into equal parts of ninety degrees each. Zeros have no numerical value so we eliminate them, leaving four equal parts of nine, or 4 x 9 = 36. Thirty-six then is the starting point for figuring the pinnacles. To determine the first pinnacle, we subtract the Destiny number (complete birthdate reduced to a digit) from 36.

29

In the example we used heretofore, the full birthdate was July 14, 1950, or $7 + 5 + 6 = 18 = 9$ Destiny. $36-9 = 27$ so the first pinnacle applies from birth to age 27. The second and third pinnacles cover nine-year periods each, thus age 28 to 37 is the second pinnacle, and age 38 to 47 the third pinnacle for this birthdate. The fourth and last pinnacle remains in effect for the balance of this lifetime.

In composing a chart we show the pinnacles by building upright pyramids over the digits of the birthdate following these rules:

1st pinnacle: Add the digit of the month to the digit of the day of birth.

2nd pinnacle: Add the digit of the day to the digit of the year.

3rd pinnacle: Add together the first and second pinnacles.

4th pinnacle: Add together the digits of the month and year of birth.

Still using the birthdate July 14, 1950, we proceed as follows:

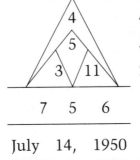

4	4th pinnacle
5	3rd pinnacle
1st pinnacle   3 11   2nd pinnacle

7   5   6

July   14,   1950

$7 + 5 + 6 = 18 = 9$ Destiny
$36 - 9 = 27$

Birth to age 27	1st pinnacle 3
28 to age 37	2nd pinnacle 11
38 to age 47	3rd pinnacle 5
48 on	4th pinnacle 4

Consult the list showing the general number vibrations (page 9) in order to interpret the influences of the four pinnacles in this or any chart.

In the above chart the 9 Destiny shows this individual possesses leadership and independence. His first pinnacle (3), self-expression, suggests he will decide early in life to indulge in some form of activity which will place him in the limelight (2nd pinnacle 11). His 9 Destiny (universal number) indicates he could be occupied with something which will necessitate much travel

and change (3rd pinnacle 5). In his last pinnacle
(4) he will be inclined to settle down to a more
staid and practical progression.

Here are a few additional suggestions concerning the positions of some of the pinnacle numbers.

If Three (self-expression) is found as a first pinnacle, it may be wasted as youth is inclined to
play and have fun and so may miss opportunities
for serious self-expression.

If Four (practicality) is a first pinnacle, it
denotes the individual is forced to work and be
practical at an early age when youth is not yet
prepared to be saddled with heavy responsibility.

If Seven (perfection) appears as an early pinnacle, it may cause a rift with a marriage partner or
other close relationship because the individual is
inclined to be critical or uncommunicative.

Nine as an early pinnacle could foreshadow a
divorce or other negative condition as it is an
ending vibration. It may also indicate a complete
change of endeavor to a new field of expression.

THE CHALLENGES

"Challenges to meet—
   like seasonings in our foods
      tests are spice of life!"

As road blocks are set up to detain traffic, so challenges are employed along the time track of our lives to test our mettle, incite interest, demand attention or force action.

We use the digits of the birthdate as we did with the Pinnacles to determine the Challenges. However, we apply subtraction instead of addition observing the following rules:

1. Subtract the digit of the month and the digit of the day from each other.
2. Subtract the digit of the day and the digit of the year from each other.
3. Subtract the two remaining numbers from each other.
4. Subtract the digit of the month and the digit of the year from each other.

To illustrate we build an inverted pyramid using the same birthdate as before, July 14, 1950, thus:

July   14,   1950
────────────────────────
7   5   6   (9 Destiny)

1st challenge   2   1   2nd challenge

3rd challenge   1
  (main)   1   4th challenge

The individual whose birthday is July 14, 1950, has as a first challenge, the Two which indicates he must learn to cooperate with others using tact and diplomacy. His Nine Destiny tells us he is a leader, independent, who wants to do things his own way without interference, so his Two challenge says he *must learn* to cooperate with others. The remaining challenges being Ones suggest he must stand on his own two feet maintaining his independence but must avoid being domineering. His main challenge being a One cautions him to handle his dominance gracefully in dealing with others. The first and second challenges usually apply to youth or the early years of life, while the third, or main, challenge is handled in adult life. If the fourth and last challenge is different than the earlier ones, it suggests an added test in the latter years of life.

The challenges may easily be interpreted by consulting the list under general Interpretation of

Number vibrations (page 9). There are a few numbers, however, that need special mention.

If Zero appears as a challenge, it indicates an old, old soul. It also poses a possible one of two situations: Either the individual has many obstacles to overcome, or he has none. Only he can answer this.

If Six appears as one or more of the challenges, it indicates an individual who is opinionated, thinking he or his attitude is absolutely correct. He is inclined to adhere stubbornly to this tenet and must learn to allow for others' opinions. Also he must learn to assume responsibility.

A Seven challenge may foreshadow a serious, often traumatic experience, especially since the victim is inclined to give up and make no effort to overcome the problem.

An Eight challenge indicates a strong desire for material success in which the individual concerned often wishes to outdo his associates and become "Top Man" while denying the same privilege to others. He must learn that others, if they make similar efforts for gains, are also entitled to the rewards.

THE DESTINY NUMBER

"The Destiny Map
    defines highroad to success–
        ignore the detours!"

So important to each individual is the Destiny number (total birthdate reduced to a digit) that unless otherwise interfered with in some manner, an infant will not arrive in this world until the vibrations are perfect for its debut. Unfortunately, sometimes doctors or unforeseen circumstances force delivery prematurely. This burdens a newborn with added problems to cope with in its sojourn here.

The Destiny number is the strongest, most important influence in one's chart. It sets the pace for each individual's endeavors in this particular life experience. There are no two of us exactly alike. Each is unique and each has inherited some special talent or inclination for expressing himself in his own way to the best of his ability at his present state of development. He must seek out this innate quality and put it to work for his own progress. Knowing and understanding his Destiny number will aid him in recognizing his propensities. The sooner he puts his own deep desires to work, the more rapid will be his progress toward success and happiness.

Unfortunately, many become discouraged and fall by the wayside before they realize how really special they are. For instance, our schools have many drop-outs. A young man may leave school early, marry and acquire a family which he is obligated to support. He takes a job, any job, in order to support himself and family. He hates his work because he is not doing the thing he came here to accomplish. But he is not trained or prepared for his real role in life and fears to give up a job which supports himself and family. Inwardly he resents his situation and over a period of time psychosomatic illness takes its toll. The only answer is to ferret out your innate abilites and work toward learning and perfecting what must be done to put these natural attributes into operation.

Special qualities accrue to each Destiny number as follows:

Destiny No. 1. Independence. Self-motivation. Self-reliance. Invention. Activity. Force. Ambition. The pioneer exploring new fields of endeavor. Originality. Creativity. Individuality. Ones are strong leaders. In their quest for independence, they must avoid being domineering, selfish, egotistical and overconfident.

Destiny No. 2. Cooperation. Diplomacy. Persuasiveness. Peace-makers and Arbitrators. Good mixers. Work well with groups. Twos are often inclined to be reticent, too sensitive and timid, which they must work to overcome.

Destiny No. 3. Self-expression. Creative. Artistic. Imaginative. Sensitive. Versatile. Affable. Good mixers socially as they like fun and people. Have sense of humor. Intuitive. Changeable. Threes may be in high spirits one moment and in depths of depression the next.

Destiny No. 4. Practicality. Organization. Dependability. Down-to-earth hard workers. Concentrate and work out details well. Sometimes a Four Destiny is so busy watching where his feet are going he misses spiritual values. A Four Spiritual Birthday eases a rough Four vibration.

Destiny No. 5. Freedom. Activity. Travel. Adventure. Progress. Changeability. Versatility. Charm. Make excellent salesmen with their charming personalities. Fives insist on being free to think and act as they see fit. Because many lines of endeavor come easily to them, they may waste efforts by indulging in too many varied activities. Must learn to concentrate on the few most important undertakings.

Destiny No. 6. Love. Home. Domesticity. Service. Responsibility. Musical talents. Six is the love number, a beautiful home and family as well as community vibration. Sixes usually work for the improvement of their surroundings. Unfortunately, a Six is inclined to be extremely opinionated. Must learn that others in a different position may see the same problem in a different light. A Six must learn to make allowances for the opinions of others. Sometimes a Six Destiny may be inclined to manipulate others for his own gains. Six is the Money number of the Air sign.

Destiny No. 7. Spirituality. Specialization. Research. Study. Analytical. Secretive. Wisdom. Silence. Aloof, a loner. Brilliant but uncommunicative. Sevens are not inclined to reveal their innermost thoughts, but mull over facts in their own minds to reach a decision but are still prone to remain silent. Need time to be alone for meditation, analyzing and reaching decisions.

Destiny No. 8. Harvest number. Business. Finance. Authority. Management. Executive ability. Material success. Practical. Efficient. Eights stress material gains. Must not lose sight of spiritual values while seeking material success. A Trinity number.

Destiny No. 9. Universalists. Leaders. Humanitarians. Idealists. Philanthropy. Service. Optimism. Drive. Independence. Sensitive and sympathetic. Intuitive. A Trinity number. Must work for the betterment of others. Nines may indulge in travel, communications and foreign fields of service. Capable of great accomplishments often world wide. Nine being the top digit indicates a completion vibration. In any calculation the number nine does not alter the ultimate number.

Destiny No. 11. Idealism. Diplomacy. Cooperation. Inspiration. Intuition. Invention. Eleven is the idealist, a cooperative, diplomatic nature and a candidate for the limelight easily performing in some capacity before the public. Eleven is a Master number and a Trinity number. Eleven is an ideal marriage partner as it is inspirational, diplomatic and cooperative.

The Master Eleven (as well as Twenty-two) is sometimes elusive when determining the Destiny number. For instance, the birthdate August 23, 1942, elicits the digits

$$8 + 5 + 7 = 20 = 2$$

Now take $8 + 5 = 13 = 4$. $4 + 7 = 11$. This we term a weak Eleven. If the individual to whom this belongs does not expend the effort to use the strong Master Eleven influence, it reverts to the lesser Two. However, the Eleven potential exists.

Destiny No. 22. Practical Idealist. Master Builder. Twenty-two, a double Eleven, is idealistic but also practical. The combination adds up to Master Builder. This strong vibration can accomplish whatever it desires. Since a Four day in the Spiritual Calendar is the Spiritual Birthday for a Twenty-two Destiny, it affords protection not accorded to others in a Four vibration.

As with the Eleven Destiny above, Twenty-two Destinies sometimes evade detection. For example, February 8, 1947, shows the digits

$$2 + 8 + 3 = 13 = 4$$

If we calculate in this manner:

$$
\begin{array}{rl}
1947 & - \text{ year} \\
8 & - \text{ day} \\
2 & - \text{ month} \\
\hline
1957 & \\
\hline
22 &
\end{array}
$$

we reveal the hidden Twenty-two which we do not reduce.

While 11, 22 and 33 are termed Master numbers, 8, 9 *and 11* Destiny numbers are called Trinity numbers. They emanate special highly spiritual vibrations. Any one of these as a Destiny number should be highly acclaimed and appreciated. The Trinity signifies completeness.

Various aspects of the Trinity:

1. Father, Mother, Son.
2. Father, Son, Holy Spirit.
3. Physical, Mental, Spiritual.
4. Body, Mind, Soul.
5. Mind, Idea, Manifestation.
6. Conscious, Subconscious, Superconscious.
7. Consciousness, Thought, Whole Picture.
8. Time, Space, Patience.

Symbols for the Trinity numbers are as follows:

8 – Two circles, one atop the other. Upper circle is all-inclusive, the Cosmos, God. Lower circle represents the material, physical world. The combination spells spiritual and material success.

9—Cosmic circle combined with One. The One indicates a beginning, while the circle designates attainment or completion. All numbers, 1 to 9, included.

11—Two strong Ones supporting and intensifying each other. Idealism. Peace. Inspiration. Diplomacy.

In seeking marriage alliances or other close and intimate partnerships, the most ideal situations exist if the Destiny numbers of those concerned stand side by side. If there is too wide a separation in Destiny numbers, there is likely to be a lack of understanding which, of course, may presage conflicts. If the Destiny numbers coincide, the parties involved will have a great deal in common including understanding of each other. Ofttimes, however, in this situation each may strive to be the leader or boss, which can create problems.

The least compatible combination for marriage is between members of the Water and Fire signs. Such alliances should be strictly avoided unless both parties are advanced enough to deal sensibly with differences.

THE MAGIC IN NAMES

EXPRESSION, AMBITION, IMPRESSION, REALITY OR POWER NUMBER, TEMPERAMENT

"Magic hides in names—
like story books, names tell tales
that lead to riches!"

There's magic in names, romance in names. Names tell tales, reveal secrets, furnish aid. Many years ago in San Francisco I listened to a lecture by Neville, a prolific metaphysical writer and lecturer who authored such books as *Feeling is the Secret, Out of this World,* and many more. I recall vividly a statement he made concerning names. He said parents seldom fail to give a newborn babe its rightful name befitting its role in life even though they are not aware of doing so. So important is the given name in designating the path each individual is to follow in this life's sojourn that usually parents unknowingly select a name with the needed vibrations to further the child's progress.

The letters in names vibrate to numbers as shown in the alphabet on pages 4 and 50. Your name (given name at birth to which you will vibrate throughout this lifetime) denotes your *Expression* number, the pathway mapped out for you in this life span. It also reveals your *Ambition* or *Heart's Desire* (total of vowels in name). It shows how you appear to others, known as the *Impression* or *Personality* number (total of consonants in name). Your *Destiny* (total of birthdate) is the most important number in your chart, the second in importance being your *Expression* number (total vibrations in given name) and third in value, called your *Reality* or *Power* number, is the result obtained by adding together the Destiny and Expression numbers. This third or Reality number becomes more powerful as you advance in years.

The name also provides the clue to each individual's temperament. To determine the strength of one's mental, emotional, physical and intuitive qualities, we list the numbers of Ones through Nines (see chart on page 53) appearing in the full given name. *Ones* and *Eights* divulge mental vibrations. *Twos*, *Threes*, and *Sixes* denote emotional tendencies; *Fours* and *Fives* physical stamina, and *Sevens* and *Nines* intuitive qualities. If one or more of each vibration appears in the complete name, no special problems are posed. If many numbers are missing, however, this does evoke problems (indicates Karmic tests) unless the missing vibrations are found in other strong positions in the chart. If not, we must select an additional name that will supply at least some of the missing vibrations and still respond to the Money or Success number in the signature. If many units appear in any of the four positions, it adds strength to the quality of the vibrations.

Another point to consider when building a chart concerns the letter ''Y'' in names. In calculating the Ambition number (vowels) the letter ''Y'' sometimes acts as a vowel if it is the only vowel sound in the first syllable of a name such as Sylvia, Sybil, Cyril, Cyrus, etc. However, if the Ambition and Impression numbers do not seem to be compatible with the overall character of the individual when placing the ''Y'' as a vowel, then it remains a consonant. Each individual will recognize whether or not to place ''Y'' as a vowel in these instances.

CHART CONSTRUCTION
AND ANALYSIS

"First chart your life path—
then adhere to basic plans
until goals are reached."

The key points in any chart are first the Destiny number, then Expression, Reality, Ambition, Impression and Temperament. Other numbers play supporting roles. Since so many of the Key points in a chart show up in the name, we are ready to set up a chart for practice and analysis.

For example, the first chart selected for analysis is that of Dr. Frederick Reindel Smith, an Osteopath and M.D. who has already mastered many of the propositions set up for him at birth. Besides, he is our very own local celebrity with worldwide affiliations as well. Note the following excerpt from our local newspaper dated December 19, 1979: "HONOR FOR DR. FRITZ SMITH – 'Fritz' Frederick Smith, M.D., has been named a Fellow of the College of Traditional Chinese Acupuncture in the United Kingdom by J. W. Worsley, president.

"Dr. Smith, who practices Acupuncture in Watsonville, was honored for his exceptional work in establishing the standards of the college in the State of California and for his assistance to the numerous students in that state in their process of seeking certification and a legal situation in which to practice."

Furthermore, he is one of the most advanced practitioners in the field of holistic health, acupuncture and acupressure in this area, a fabulous individual who is making giant strides in aiding scores of people on the path to improved living mentally, emotionally and physically as well as spiritually. Dr. Smith is known affectionately to his friends and patients as "Dr. Fritz."

To facilitate working out Dr. Smith's chart, we will again list the alphabet with its corresponding numbers:

1	2	3	4	5	6	7	8	9
A	B	C	D	E	F	G	H	I
J	K	L	M	N	O	P	Q	R
S	T	U	V	W	X	Y	Z	&

In contemplating the chart of "Dr. Fritz," we first note the strong One Destiny number revealing independence, self-reliance, self-motivation, the pioneer exploring new or advanced fields of endeavor. His birthday being an Eleven day places him in the Fire sign, an excellent business vibration. His early life being very active (5 major cycle) together with Seven for a first pinnacle shows study, research, analysis and perfection in his work. His second pinnacle (5) denotes continued activity and travel. He assumes his place in the limelight easily and naturally (11 Ambition) teaching and lecturing. His Expression number (8) being the harvest number as well as the Money or Success number of his Fire sign assures material success, while his Impression or Personality number (6) shows responsibility and a person with whom it is easy to communicate. His Reality number (9) being the universal number confirms that he deals with the many and also indicates he is capable of great accomplishments.

The most important number in his chart is the powerful ONE Destiny (independence, self-reliance, etc.); then the EIGHT Expression (material success as well as the Money or Success number of his Fire sign—born on 11 day). Third in value is his Reality or Power number NINE (universalism, capable of great accomplishments).

His Temperament chart shows only one letter vibration missing (7) which is supplied in his name "Frederick" (7) as well as his nickname "Fritz" (7). This portion of the chart shows him to be exceptionally strong physically (8 points) and highly intuitive (6 points) which indicates a high degree of empathy with his patients.

Dr. FREDERICK REINDEL SMITH

Born $\underline{\text{May}}$ $\underline{11,}$ $\underline{1929}$

$\quad$ 5 $\;+\;$ 2 $\;+\;$ 3 $\;= 10 = 1$ Destiny, Fire sign
$\qquad\qquad\qquad\qquad$ (born 11/2 day)

1981 Personal Year $= 8$ (1981 year 1 + month 5 +
$\qquad\qquad\qquad\qquad\qquad\qquad$ day 11/2)

Major Cycles:

$\quad$ 1929 to 1956, 1st cycle – 5
$\quad$ (to age 27 years, 1st cycle, ruled by month of birth)

$\quad$ 1956 to 1983, 2nd cycle – 11/2
$\quad$ (27 to 54 years, 2nd cycle, ruled by day of birth)

$\quad$ 1983 on $\quad\quad$, 3rd cycle – 3
$\quad$ (54 years on, 3rd cycle, ruled by year of birth)

$\dfrac{1}{19}$	$+$	$\dfrac{1}{19}$	$+$	$\dfrac{9}{9}$	$= 11$ *Ambition*
5 5 9		59 5		9	(vowels)

FREDERICK	REINDEL	SMITH
695459932	9595453	14928
$\dfrac{52}{7}$	$\dfrac{40}{4}$	$\dfrac{24}{6}$

$\quad$ 7 $\;+\;$ 4 $\;+\;$ 6 $\quad = 17/8$ *Expression*
$\qquad\qquad\qquad\qquad\qquad\qquad$ (total digits
$\qquad\qquad\qquad\qquad\qquad\qquad$ in name)

69 4 9 32	9 54 3	14 28
$\dfrac{33}{6}$	$\dfrac{21}{3}$	$\dfrac{15}{6}$

$\quad$ 6 $\;+\;$ 3 $\;+\;$ 6 $\quad = 15/6$ *Impression*
$\qquad\qquad\qquad\qquad\qquad\qquad$ (consonants)

Destiny	1	Fritz
Expression	8	69928
	—	——
		34
Reality or Power	9	7

TEMPERAMENT

Number of:

1s	1	1s, 8s	Mental	2
2s	2	2, 3, 6	Emotional	5
3s	2	4, 5	Physical	8
4s	3	7, 9	Intuitive	6
5s	5			—
6s	1			21
7s	0			
8s	1			
9s	6			
	—			
	21			

```
              8        4th pinnacle
             /3\       3rd pinnacle
1st pinnacle/7 \5\     2nd pinnacle
           /___\/___\

       5    2    3
      /____\/____\
1st challenge\3/ \1/   2nd challenge
3rd challenge \2/
  (main)      2        4th challenge
```

36 – 1 = 35

Birth to age 35	–	1st pinnacle 7
36 to age 45	–	2nd pinnacle 5
46 to age 55	–	3rd pinnacle 3
56 on	–	4th pinnacle 8

In scanning the Doctor's Challenges we see his first Challenge is a Three (self-expression) which tells us that early in life he made up his mind concerning the path he wished to follow. The second challenge (1, independence) indicates that he learned in his youth to be self-reliant while his main challenge (2) shows that he has acquired tact and diplomacy in dealing with all types of people.

"Dr. Fritz" is now in his third pinnacle (a 3) which is self-expression. I know he is working on a book at this time in addition to an already extremely busy schedule. His final pinnacle (8) assures continued material success, while his final major cycle (3) indicates continued mental and spiritual growth and satisfaction. He is in an Eight Personal Year in 1981 (harvest number). I do not doubt that he will have his book ready for publication in 1983, his next strong One Personal Year.

The Doctor's life and accomplishments to date show he has followed and used to advantage the vibrations indicated by the various numbers appearing in his chart.

The most impressive chart I have ever encountered is that of a Psychic, Georgia M. Hughes, located in New York, who has the three Master numbers 11, 22, and 33, in the most important positions in her chart, plus additional Master numbers 11 and 22 in secondary spots.

Georgia is a dynamic, youthful looking individual with blue, wide open, intense, sparkling eyes and lovely skin that belies her fifty years.

For your perusal I shall list her chart because, like "Dr. Fritz," she has "lived" the numbers in her chart beautifully and fully. Georgia has not only reared six children of her own but several orphaned nieces and nephews, making a total of seventeen altogether, a monumental task. She certainly has demonstrated her Twenty-two Expression number (Master Builder) and still retains her youthful vim and vigor as she continues to serve others. Currently she periodically accompanies an exploratory expedition group to Yucatan in search of Mayan records.

In analyzing Georgia's chart, we first note her Eleven Destiny (a Trinity number) which tells us she belongs in the limelight, is diplomatic, cooperative, tactful, idealistic and an inspiration to others. Her first major cycle (2) indicates a partnership (early marriage) while her second major cycle (22) together with her Expression number (also 22) makes her capable of great accomplishments, evidenced by the successful rearing of seventeen children, a phenomenal undertaking. Her Eleven Ambition and Eleven Impression numbers indicate she accepts the limelight easily and naturally, while her Thirty-three Reality or

GEORGIA MARTHA
VILLNAVE (HUGHES)

Signature:

Georgia   M.   Hughes
—————   ——   ——————
  8   + 4 +   5   = 17/8

Born Feb 22, 1931
      ——— ——— ————
       2 + 4 + 5   = 11 Destiny, Fire sign
                          (born 22/4 day)

1981 Personal Year = 7 (1981 year 1 + month 2 +
                                  day 22/4)

Major Cycles:

   1931 to 1957, 1st cycle – 2
   (birth to 26 years ruled by month of birth)

   1957 to 1984, 2nd cycle – 22/4
   (26 to 53 years, ruled by day of birth)

   1984 on   , 3rd cycle – 5
   (ruled by year of birth)

     3   +   2   +   6   = 11 *Ambition*
     ——   —   ——   *(vowels)*
     21   2   15
     ——   —   ——
    5 6   9 1   1   1   9   1 5
   ————————   ————————   ————————   ————————
   GEORGIA   MARTHA   VILLNAVE   (HUGHES)
   ————————   ————————   ————————   ————————
   7569791   419281   49335145   837851
     ——   ——   ——   ——
     44   25   34   32/5
     ——   ——   ——
     8   +   7   +   7   = 22 *Expression*
                                          (total digits
                                           in name)
    7   97   4 928   4 335 4   + 5 (Hughes)
   ————————   ————————   ————————
     23   23   19
     ——   ——   ——
     5   +   5   +   1   = 11 *Impression*
                                          (consonants)

Destiny	11
Expression	22
Reality or Power	33

TEMPERAMENT

Number of:

1s	4	1s, 8s	Mental	5
2s	1	2, 3, 6	Emotional	4
3s	2	4, 5	Physical	6
4s	3	7, 9	Intuitive	6
5s	3			—
6s	1			21
7s	2			
8s	1			
9s	4			
	—			
	21			

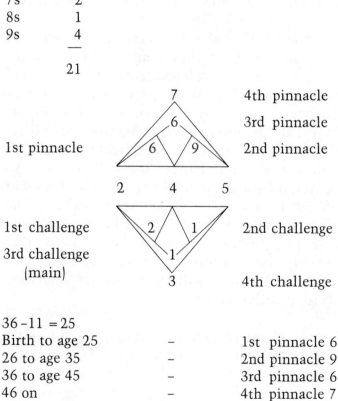

		7	4th pinnacle
		6	3rd pinnacle
1st pinnacle		6 9	2nd pinnacle
	2	4 5	

1st challenge	2 1	2nd challenge
3rd challenge (main)	1	
	3	4th challenge

36 – 11 = 25

Birth to age 25	–	1st pinnacle 6
26 to age 35	–	2nd pinnacle 9
36 to age 45	–	3rd pinnacle 6
46 on	–	4th pinnacle 7

Power number shows a high degree of spirituality confirmed by her psychic ability.

Temperamentally she is very well balanced with all vibrations plentifully supplied, particularly strong physically (6 points) and highly endowed intuitively (6 points) psychic ability.

Georgia's first Pinnacle deals with the home (6), the rearing of children which was completed in her Second Pinnacle (9) and a branching out to aid others (3rd Pinnacle 6) while her final Pinnacle (7) where she stands now is a spiritual vibration like her Thirty-three Reality number.

Georgia's first challenge (2) tells us that early in life she learned to be diplomatic and cooperative as well as acquiring independence of thought and action (2nd and 3rd challenges 1s) while her final challenge (3, self-expression) confirms her present activity, aiding others through her psychic ability.

Her final Major Cycle (5) indicates continued activity, travel and change. She will continue to be active for the balance of her life. Her Personal Year, 1981, is a Seven which shows delays. She has been experiencing delays in her travel plans due in part to the Airlines' Controllers' strike. However, she is approaching an Eight Personal year in 1982 which will speed up her activities with its positive vibes.

I now suggest you set up your own chart following the plans for Dr. Smith's and Mrs. Hughes' charts.

You already know the *Day* of birth determines the *Sign* you are in. The complete birthdate digit gives you the all-important *Destiny* number. You arrive at the dates for the *Major Cycles* by finding the nearest *One Personal Year* to twenty-five year periods. The given name at birth indicates your *Expression* number while the *Vowels* reveal your *Ambition* or *Heart's Desire* and the *Consonants* your *Impression* or *Personality* picture. The *Reality* or *Power* number is the combination of the *Destiny* and *Expression* numbers. The birth digits with upright pyramids depict the Pinnacles (helpful highlights), while the inverted pyramids point out Challenges (tests). The *Temperament* is discovered by counting the numbers of *Ones* through *Nines* in the full given name at birth. Your *Current Personal Year* is determined by adding the digit of the *present world year* to the digits of your *month* and *day* of birth.

Refer to the "Interpretation of Number Vibrations" (on page 9) and "The Destiny Number" (page 37) to analyze and understand your own *Destiny* and the path you should follow to attain the greatest personal success. Your numeroscope will, no doubt, cause you to appreciate and respect your own unique individuality and will inspire you to improve your present and future situations along life's highway.

THE MONEY OR SUCCESS NUMBER

"Money" and "Success"—
twins who travel side by side,
think and act alike."

Money is a symbol for success in our material world. The Money number of numerology when applied to our signature enhances our potential for success in a most powerful and fascinating manner. For instance, when we sign our name on a check with the total of its vibrations responding to our money number, this money going into circulation is helping someone. Through our thinking, what we send out returns to us in kind. This is the simple operation of the mind. As Shakespeare so aptly put it in *Hamlet*: "Nothing's either good or bad but thinking makes it so." When our signature vibrates to our money or success number and we realize or acknowledge this in our minds the returns can be fabulous. We open floodgates to success.

How do we apply this money number to our signature? It is simple but powerful.

There is a special money number for each sign. *Five* is the money or success vibration for the *Water* sign. *Eight* is the the money number for the *Fire* sign. *Six* is the money number for *Air* subjects.

If the signature you are presently using does not vibrate to the proper money number for its sign, you then find an additional name to incorporate in the signature to provide this desired vibration. Sometimes a change in spelling of a name does the trick as we shall show later. With the selection of the appropriate additional name, the total of the full name should respond to your money number. Also to facilitate matters, if the proper selection has been worked out, we should be able to use only middle initials in writing the signature and still maintain the proper vibrations.

To simplify the application of the proper digits to letters in a name, we will repeat the alphabet with its digits:

1	2	3	4	5	6	7	8	9
A	B	C	D	E	F	G	H	I
J	K	L	M	N	O	P	Q	R
S	T	U	V	W	X	Y	Z	&

Now let's consider the hypothetical name Mary Alice Miller. To illustrate we will assume Mary's *birthday* places her in the Water sign. Five is the money number of the water sign but Mary Alice Miller vibrates to Three, thus:

Mary	Alice	Miller
4 197	13935	4 93359
21	21	33
3 +	3 +	6 = 12 = 3

We wish to retain the "A" in Alice, thus:

$$\text{Mary} \quad \text{A.} \quad \text{Miller}$$
$$3 \quad + 1 + \quad 6 \quad = 10 = 1$$

To this result of 1 we must now add 4 to give her the money number of the Water sign which is 5.

$$\text{Mary} \quad \text{A.} \quad \text{D.} \quad \text{Miller}$$
$$3 \quad + 1 + 4 + \quad 6 \quad = 14 = 5$$

Since there are three letters that vibrate to 4, (D, M, V) any one of these may be used, so to complete her full name so that it, too, vibrates to her money number, we discover that Alice vibrates to *three*, thus

$$\text{Mary} \quad \text{Alice} \quad \text{D ?} \quad \text{Miller}$$
$$3 \quad + \quad 3 \quad + 2 + \quad 6 \quad = 14 = 5$$

Now we must find a name beginning with "D" (or M or V) which vibrates to *two*, thus

$$\underline{\text{M a r y}} \quad \underline{\text{A l i c e}} \quad \underline{\text{D o r a}} \quad \underline{\text{M i l l e r}}$$
$$4\,6\,9\,1$$
$$3 \quad + \quad 3 \quad + \quad 2 \quad + \quad 6 \quad = 14 = 5$$

As mentioned earlier, sometimes a change in the spelling of a name will work out satisfactorily as,

$$\underline{\text{M a r i a l i c e}} \quad \underline{\text{M i l l e r}}$$
$$4\,19913935 \quad 4\,93359$$
$$\underline{44} \quad + \quad \underline{33}$$
$$8 \quad + \quad 6 \quad = 14 = 5$$

In any public library you may find books listing boys' and girls' names. Checking the number vibrations of the alphabet, you then experiment to find the required name with the correct vibration.

To further illustrate working out the money number, let us still use the same name, Mary Alice Miller, but let us now assume that Mary's *birthday* places her in the Fire sign. Her money number then will be *Eight*. In this instance with

$$\underline{\text{M a r y}} \quad \underline{\text{A.}} \quad \underline{?} \quad \underline{\text{M i l l e r}}$$
$$3 \quad + 1 + 7 + \quad 6 \quad = 17 = 8$$

We need the seven to give her name the money number 8 of the Fire sign. The letters that vibrate to seven are G, P and Y, thus one of these letters will suffice like

$$\underline{\text{M a r y}} \quad \underline{\text{A.}} \quad \underline{\text{P.}} \quad \underline{\text{M i l l e r}}$$
$$3 \quad + \ 1 \ + \ 7 \ + \quad 6 \quad = 17 = 8$$

Also:

$$\underline{\text{M a r y}} \quad \underline{\text{A l i c e}} \quad \underline{\text{P a t r i c i a}} \quad \underline{\text{M i l l e r}}$$
$$\underline{7 1 2 9 9 3 9 1}$$
$$\underline{4 1}$$
$$3 \quad + \quad 3 \quad + \quad 5 \quad + \quad 6 \quad = 17 = 8$$

We may also gain the desired results by changing the spelling of Alice, thus:

$$\underline{\text{M a r y}} \quad \underline{\text{A l y c e}} \quad \underline{\text{M i l l e r}}$$
$$\underline{1 3 7 3 5}$$
$$\underline{1 7}$$
$$3 \quad + \quad 8 \quad + \quad 6 \quad = 17 = 8$$

Again, using the same name, Mary Alice Miller, let us now assume Mary's *birthday* places her in the Air sign with Six as the money number of the Air.

$$\frac{\text{Mary} \quad \text{Alice} \quad \text{Miller}}{3 \quad + \quad 3 \quad + \quad 6} \quad = 12 = 3$$

Retaining the "A" in Alice we have

$$\frac{\text{Mary} \quad \text{A.} \quad \text{Miller}}{3 \quad + 1 + \quad 6} \quad = 10 = 1$$

We need to add *five* to bring the total to Six. The letters E, N and W vibrate to *five* thus,

$$\frac{\text{Mary} \quad \text{A.} \quad \text{E.} \quad \text{Miller}}{3 \quad + 1 + 5 + \quad 6} \quad = 15 = 6$$

or

$$\frac{\text{Mary} \quad \text{Alice} \quad \frac{\text{Esther}}{\frac{512859}{30}} \quad \text{Miller}}{3 \quad + \quad 3 \quad + \quad 3 \quad + \quad 6} \quad = 15 = 6$$

Therefore using first and last names with initials A and E as well as the full name as shown above, gives her the Six vibration for success.

Remember Five is the money or success number for the Water sign, Eight for Fire and Six for Air. The application of this success vibration to your signature enhances your possibilities. Do not delay putting it into practice. Your own mind is standing by to help you. Your subconscious and superconscious will find the means to promote your interests if you request the aid. Give it this added incentive and use your Spiritual Birthdays to seek its help. I have witnessed phenomenal results within short periods of time after employing this influence in the signature. This is one of the most feasible aspects in the use of numerology.

If more than *Three* number vibrations are missing in your given name at birth, you should seek an additional name that will supply at least one or more of the missing letters and still maintain the money or success vibration in your signature. Three Zeros in your given name is the maximum that should be permitted to remain. Missing letters indicate Karmic conditions that may place obstacles in your pathway.

SPIRITUAL BIRTHDAYS
and the
SPIRITUAL CALENDAR

"Golden dreams come true—
our Spiritual Birthdays
are the catalysts!"

Two of the most intriguing and helpful aspects in numerology are the vibrations of numbers in the Universal or Spiritual Calendar and your Spiritual Birthdays. When you put these powerful influences to work for you, the results can be fantastic. Your Spiritual Birthdays will teach you the true meaning of "magic." There is no other word that identifies with the working of this influence so aptly as "magic." It is the "Open Sesame" to success.

Before you can determine your Spiritual Birthday, you must first understand the Spiritual Calendar. To calculate the Spiritual Calendar, let's start with the year 1981. Add the digits of the year:

$$1 + 9 + 8 + 1 = 19$$
$$1 + 9 = 10$$
$$1 + 0 = 1$$

This tells us that 1981 is a One World year. To this number 1 year add 1 for January, the first month, plus 1 for the first day of January, thus $1 + 1 + 1 = 3$. This indicates the first day of January, 1981, is a 3 day in the Spiritual Calendar. Now continue marking the days immediately following 4, 5, 6, 7, 8, 9. Since 9 is the top digit, we continue to mark the balance of the days for January from 1 to 9, then repeating to the last day. This gives us the spiritual vibrations for the month of January, 1981.

REGULAR AND SPIRITUAL CALENDARS FOR JANUARY 1981

	Sun	Mon	Tue	Wed	Thu	Fri	Sat
Regular					1	2	3
Spiritual					3	4	5
Regular	4	5	6	7	8	9	10
Spiritual	6	7	8	9	1	2	3
Regular	11	12	13	14	15	16	17
Spiritual	4	5	6	7	8	9	1
Regular	18	19	20	21	22	23	24
Spiritual	2	3	4	5	6	7	8
Regular	25	26	27	28	29	30	31
Spiritual	9	1	2	3	4	5	6

Now calculate February, 1981, in the same manner we did for January, 1981: to the 1 year add 2 for February and 1 for the first day of February, thus:

$$1 + 2 + 1 = 4$$

making February 1, 1981, a 4 day in the Spiritual Calendar. Continue marking the following days 5 to 9, then repeating 1 to 9 for the balance of days in February. Use this method for the entire year, always starting with the first day of the month.

The months are numbered as follows:

January	1	July	7
February	2	August	8
March	3	September	9
April	4	October	10 or 1
May	5	November	11 or 2
June	6	December	12 or 3

To quickly calculate the vibration of any particular day in the Spiritual Calendar if your marked calendar is not handy, just add the numbers of the current year, current month and current day, reducing the total to a digit. This gives the spiritual vibration for that day.

When you have marked the calendar showing the spiritual vibrations for each day, refer to the chapter on "Interpretation of Number Vibrations" (pages 9–15) to aid you in understanding the influences at work on any particular day so that you may guide your activities accordingly. When you do this you will be surprised at the ease and satisfaction in your progress. Work becomes a joy instead of a chore or drudgery. Worries vanish and rewards increase. When the vibrations are positive, you will step up your efforts and when you recognize negative influences, you will take things in stride, cease to worry and just wait for more positive vibrations to aid your progress.

Following are a few suggestions to apply to the various number vibrations:

1. Positive; very active; a beginning.

2. Slow; attend to details; cooperate with others to accomplish whatever is necessary.

3. Self-expression; a strong vibration; a go-ahead influence.

4. Caution; be alert; hard work vibration.

5. Very active; good for travel and change; act with confidence.

6. Positive; assume responsibility; serve and help others; good community vibration.

7. Slow; ripening tide; coast.

8. Harvest; active; business vibration.

9. Finishing tide; prepare for strong 1 to follow.

The KEY to your SPIRITUAL BIRTHDAYS is your Destiny number (total numbers in birthdate reduced to a digit). The Destiny number designates *your very special day* which is identical to the same number in the Spiritual Calendar. In other words, if Six is your Destiny number, then a Six day in the Spiritual Calendar is your Spiritual Birthday. On this day your Spiritual Storehouse is wide open for you.

At birth everything necessary for your growth, success and happiness is already contained in your Spiritual Storehouse. On your Spiritual Birthday all you need to do to obtain the required needs for complete success is to ask, to pray for, or to deeply desire whatever you wish to demonstrate in your life, be it mental, spiritual, physical or material. If this practice is performed consistently and persistently, nothing will be denied that is for the ALL GOOD.

Each Destiny number claims its own identical number in the Spiritual Calendar as its Spiritual Birthday. Since the Spiritual Birthdays embrace the digits 1 to 9, an Eleven Destiny celebrates a Two day in the Spiritual Calendar as its Spiritual Birthday, while a Twenty-two Destiny vibrates to a Four day in the Spiritual Calendar as its Spiritual Birthday. All other Destinies identify with their own number.

Do not miss or overlook a Spiritual Birthday. In some months these will occur four times while in others only three, but so *VITAL* is the *Spiritual Birthday* to each individual that it can spell the difference between success or failure. Put your Spiritual Birthdays to work for you without delay and start counting your blessings!

You now have your Tool Kit assembled. With a little practice you will acquire expertise in handling the tools. The foregoing information is a working hypothesis to guide you on the high road to success. Apply its precepts and enjoy life's challenges while you reap its rewards.

Numerology is like a charm bracelet. Each individual token on the charm chain has a special meaning for the individual who wears it. So with numerology, each facet in your chart has significance and power for you. Let them charm your life path and bring their joys to you!

REMEMBER YOUR SPIRITUAL BIRTHDAYS AND WIN THE GAME OF LIFE!

WORKSHEETS

Chart Construction

Money or Success Numbers

Spiritual Calendar

Spiritual Birthday

	1	2	3	4	5	6	7	8	9
	A	B	C	D	E	F	G	H	I
	J	K	L	M	N	O	P	Q	R
	S	T	U	V	W	X	Y	Z	&

Name:

Birthdate:

Major Cycles:

Destiny

Expression

Reality or Power

TEMPERAMENT

Number of:

1s	Mental
2s	Emotional
3s	Physical
4s	Intuitive
5s	
6s	
7s	
8s	4th pinnacle
9s	3rd pinnacle
1st pinnacle	2nd pinnacle

1st challenge   2nd challenge

3rd challenge
   (main)
                                 4th challenge

36 -   =

Birth to age	–	1st pinnacle
to age	–	2nd pinnacle
to age	–	3rd pinnacle
on	–	4th pinnacle

	1	2	3	4	5	6	7	8	9
	A	B	C	D	E	F	G	H	I
	J	K	L	M	N	O	P	Q	R
	S	T	U	V	W	X	Y	Z	&

Name:

Birthdate:

Major Cycles:

Destiny

Expression

Reality or Power

TEMPERAMENT

Number of:

1s	Mental
2s	Emotional
3s	Physical
4s	Intuitive
5s	
6s	
7s	
8s	4th pinnacle
9s	3rd pinnacle
1st pinnacle	2nd pinnacle

1st challenge   2nd challenge

3rd challenge
   (main)
                                        4th challenge

36 – =		
Birth to age	–	1st pinnacle
to age	–	2nd pinnacle
to age	–	3rd pinnacle
on	–	4th pinnacle

Water Sign: born on 1, 5, or 7 day
Fire Sign: born on 2, 4, or 8 day
Air Sign: born on 3, 6, or 9 day

Signature name:

1	2	3	4	5	6	7	8	9
A	B	C	D	E	F	G	H	I
J	K	L	M	N	O	P	Q	R
S	T	U	V	W	X	Y	Z	&

(See instructions on pages 70–74)

(See instructions on pages 70–74)